Proverbs... Vol.2

German

Everyday German sayings you might not understand
By
The Secret Libraries

Translation
By
Ágnes Borbely
 YouTube

The Secret Libraries

Published by The Secret Libraries for 2017
www.theSECRETlibraries.com

Proverbs...

Proverb: A short, well-known pithy saying, stating a general truth or a piece of advice.

Idioms and proverbs define cultures and are passed down through generations. Discover more about the people, their culture and their thoughts through their traditional sayings.

This little book provides a selected collection of 111 traditional German proverbs. Have you ever had a conversation with a German where they use a strange saying to explain or react to a situation? It can be a great way to learn more about the native Germans by understanding their most popular sayings, so we have translated them and explained their meaning. And some of these are very interesting :)

Thank you for your purchase!

We spent a long time building this book we hope you enjoy it

"Da steppt der Bär."

— There steps the bear.

Meaning:

— Do you have a good feeling about a party or place you're going to? Well this phrase is the perfect way to express your excitement (Sometimes used sarcastically).

"Jeder Topf findet

seinen Deckel."

— Every pot finds its cover.

Meaning:

— There is a matching person (partner, friend ally)

for everyone.

"Ins Fettnäpfchen treten."

— To step into the fat bowl.

Meaning:

— The felling of immediately regretting something you said.

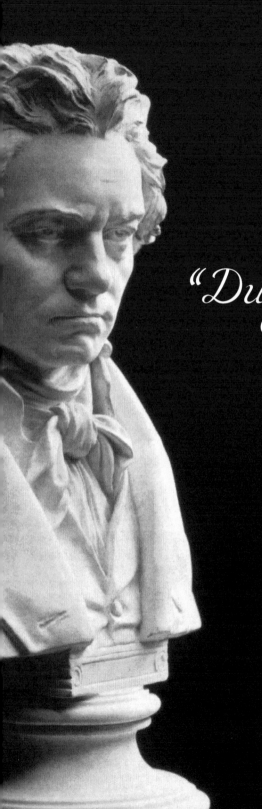

"*Du gehst mir auf den Keks.*"

— You're going on my cookie.

Meaning:

— Used when someone is really getting on your nerves.

"Warum spielst du die beleidigte Leberwurst?"

— Why are you playing the offended liver sausage?

Meaning:

— Used when someone is throwing a tantrum or overreacts to something trivial.

"Ich kriege so eine Krawatte."

—I am getting a tie.

Meaning:

—it comes from the pressure you feel in your throat when you get so angry you could scream.

"Da beisst die Maus keinen faden ab"

— The mouse doesn't bite any threads.

Meaning:

— That's how it is, you cannot change it.

"*Lieber arm dran als Arm ab.*"

— Better to be poor than have one arm less.

Meaning:

— It could be worse!

"Eine Hand wäscht die andere."

— One hand washes the other.

Meaning:

— This has the same meaning as the English proverb "You scratch my back and I'll scratch yours" – if you help someone they will return the favour.

"*Das Kind ins Wasser gefallen.*"

— The child has fallen into the water.

Meaning:

— Made a mistake that allowed something bad to happen.

"Draußen hat man hundert Augen, daheim kaum eins."

— Outside one has a hundred eyes, at home, hardly one.

Meaning:

— In the usual environment you are less attentive in every way.

"Wo der Zaun am niedrigsten is, springt jeder über."

— Where the fence is lowest, everyone jumps over.

Meaning:

— Always do things in a way that requires the absolute least amount of labour.

"Man muß die Dinge nehmen, wie sie kommen."

— One must accept things as they come.

Meaning:

— We should not plan and then try to make circumstances fit those plans. Instead we should make plans fit the circumstances.

"*Der Hund bellt und die Karawane geht vorüber.*"

– The dogs bark and the caravan moves on.

Meaning:

— Let the world say what it will.

"Wärme bringt Leben, Kälte Tod."

— Warmth brings life, coldness death.

Meaning:

— Telling the harsh truth to someone is often far less hurtful than to stay silent.

"*Die Ersten werden die Letzten sein.*"

— The first will be last.

Meaning:

— Those who are humble will be rewarded, and those who are arrogant will be humbled; Humbleness is a virtue, pride is a sin.

"*Wenn der Reiter nichts taugt, ist das Pferd schuld.*"

— If the horseman is bad, it's the horse's fault.

Meaning:

— A poor craftsman blames his tools.

"*Wer anderen eine Grube gräbt,*

fällt selbst hinein."

— Who digs a pit for others falls into it himself.

Meaning:

— If you cause harm, you will receive harm as well.

"An den Früchten erkennt man den Baum."

— You can recognise the tree form the fruit.

Meaning:

— Children often follow the example of their parents.

"Wer zuerst kommt, mahlt zuerst."

— Who comes first mills first.

Meaning:

— Those who arrive or apply earliest are most likely to get what they want from a limited supply of things. (First comes first served).

"Gleiche Gemüter suchen sich."

— Similar minds seek each other.

Meaning:

— Great minds agree.

"Wer den Kern essen will, muss die Nuss knacken."

— He that would eat the kernel must crack the nut.

Meaning:

— Nothing is achieved without effort.

"*Wer den Acker nicht will graben, der wird nicht als Unkraut haben.*"

— Who does not want to dig the land shall have nothing but weed.

Meaning:

— Nothing is achieved without effort.

"*Kümmere Dich nicht um ungelegte Eier.*"

— Don't worry about eggs that haven't been laid yet.

Meaning:

— Don't worrying about things that haven't come to pass yet and never might.

"*Wenn ein Freund bittet, so gilt nicht morgen.*"

— When a friend asks, tomorrow does not count.

Meaning:

— If your friend asks for help you will do everything you can for them.

"*Nur tote Fische schwimmen mit dem Strom.*"

— Only dead fish swim with the stream.

Meaning:

— Think for yourself rather than unquestionably follow the group.

"Eile mit Weile."

— Haste makes waste.

Meaning:

— Acting too quickly may actually slow things down but consistent, effective effort leads to success.

"*Wem nicht zu raten ist, dem ist auch nicht zu helfen.*"

— He who can't be advised, can also not be helped.

Meaning:
— Who doesn't take others advice has to help themselves.

"In der Furt soll man die Pferde nicht wechseln."

— Shouldn't change horses in midstream.

Meaning:

— It is often wise not to quit an undertaking already begun.

"*Wem das Ferkel geboten wird, soll den Sack bereit haben.*"

— The one whom the piglet is offered must keep the sack ready.

Meaning:

— We should accept the offers that has been given us.

"*Wahrheit gibt kurzen Bescheid, Lüge macht viel Redens.*"

— Truth gives a short answer, the lie makes a lot of talk.

Meaning:

— Truth is simple, lies are complicated.

"Vorrat nimmer schadet."

— Stock never hurts.

Meaning:

— An object that seems useless now may be just what you need at some future time, so do not discard it.

"Vom Regen in die Traufe."

— Out of the rain and into the eaves.

Meaning:

— Going from one unpleasant situation into one that is even worse. The idea seems to be that you are coming from the rain to stand under the edge of the eaves, where the water collected from the whole roof is going to pour onto your head.

"Viel stroh, wenig Korn."

— Much straw, little grain.

Meaning:

— Much ado about nothing.

"Aus Schaden wird man klug."

— Harm makes smart.

Meaning:

— Failure is a necessity for learning.

"*Lügen haben kurze Beine*"

— Lies have short legs.

Meaning:

— Lies will be found out quickly.

"*Taten statt Worte! or Taten sagen mehr als Wörter!*"

— Actions instead of words! or Actions speak louder than words.

Meaning:

— Practice what you preach!

"Man sieht das Hirn nicht an der Stirn."

— You don't see the brain on one's forehead.

Meaning:

— You can't judge someone at first appearance.

"*Selbst dem Teufel sein Recht geben.*"

— To give even the devil his right.

Meaning:

— If someone or something generally considered bad or undeserving has any redeeming features these should be acknowledged.

"Klappe zu, Affe tot."

— Close the lid. The monkey is dead.

Meaning:

— Let's put an end to this.

"*Schnell Urteil hat Reue feil.*"

— Hasty judgments begets remorse.

Meaning:

— A quick evaluation is a terrible evaluation.

"*Wem Gott gibt ein Amt, dem gibt er auch Verstand.*"

— Where God bestows an office, he gives brains to fill it.

Meaning:

— Someone who assumes a position of power also acts with appropriate responsibility and prudence.

"Mitgefangen, mitgehangen."

— Caught together hung together.

Meaning:

— If you go along with the crime you will be found as guilty as the criminals.

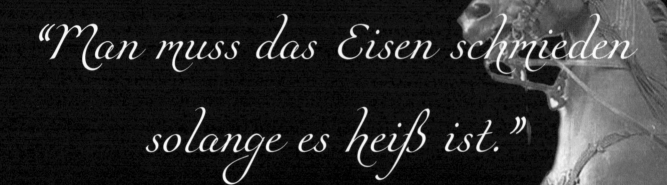

"Man muss das Eisen schmieden solange es heiß ist."

— One has to forge the iron while it is hot.

Meaning:

— You have to take advantage of immediate opportunities

"Doppelt genäht hält besser."

— Double stitched keeps better.

Meaning:

— Better safe than sorry.

"*Man kann die Natur nicht ändern.*"

— One cannot change nature.

Meaning:

— You can seldom change core human nature with the help of logic.

"Man findet bald einen Stecken, wenn man einen Hund schlagen will"

— You will soon find a stick, if you want to beat a dog.

Meaning:

— Someone who wants to be mean will find things to be mean about no matter what.

"*Keiner weiss wo dem Andern der Schuh drückt.*"

— No one knows where the shoe pinches the others.

Meaning:

— Nobody can fully understand another person's hardship or suffering.

"*Je mehr man die Katze streichelt, desto höher trägt sie den Schwanz.*"

— The more one pets the cat, the higher it holds its tail.

Meaning:

— Displaying too much affection or desperation repels your friends and love interests.

"*Im Scherz klopft man oft, und im Ernst wird auf.*"

— In a joke you often knock, and in earnest, it opens.

Meaning:

— There are a lot of true words said in a joke.

"Wem der Rock paßt, mag ihn anziehen."

— To whom the skirt fits, may wear it.

Meaning:

— Accept an unflattering, yet accurate, description of yourself.

"Hoffen und harren macht manchen

zum Narren."

— Hope and wait makes a fool of some.

Meaning:

— Do not pin all your hopes on something you may not attain, because you could end up with nothing.

"Glück bringt Neider."

— Luck brings envy.

Meaning:

—We are more angry at undeserved than at deserved good-fortune.

"Geschenk vom Feind ist

nicht gut gemeint."

— A gift from an enemy is not well-intentioned.

Meaning:

—Do not trust gifts or favours if they come from an enemy.

"*Faulheit ist der Schlüssel zur Armut.*"

— Laziness is the key to poverty.

Meaning:

— Poverty is the reward of idleness.

"*Ein gewiß ist better als zehn Ungewiß.*"

— One certainty is better than ten uncertainties.

Meaning:

— He is no wise man that will quit a certainty for an uncertainty.

"Ein Feind ist zuviel, und hundert Freunde nicht genug."

— One enemy is too many, and a hundred friends aren't enough.

Meaning:

— Do not think that one enemy is insignificant, or that you can ever have too many friends.

"Eigenlob stinkt."

— Self-praise stinks.

Meaning:

— Don't love yourself too much

"*Der Mensch denkt, Gott lenkt.*"

— Man thinks, God governs.

Meaning:

— Things often don't turn out as you would have planned.

"

"Der Schuster hat die schlechtesten Schuhe."

— The cobbler has the worst shoes.

Meaning:

— Working hard for others one may neglect one's own needs or the needs of those closest to him.

"*Jeder ist sich selbst der Nächste.*"

— Everyone is the next one to himself.

Meaning:

— Everyone will help themselves and those close to them first and then others.

"Der Horcher an der Wand hört seine eigene Schand."

— The Listener at the wall hears his own shame.

Meaning:

— People who eavesdrop on the conversations of others risk hearing unfavourable comments about themselves; used as a warning or reprimand.

"Besser ein Spatz in der Hand, als eine Taube auf dem Dach."

— A sparrow in the hand is better than a pigeon on the roof.

Meaning:

— Something you have for certain now is of more value than something better you may get, especially if you risk losing what you have in order to get it.

"*Das Glück hilft dem Kühnen.*"

— Luck helps the audacious.

Meaning:

— Those who act boldly or courageously
are most likely to succeed.

"*Auf einen groben Klotz gehört ein grober Keil.*"

— On a rough log belongs a rough wedge.

Meaning:

— One has to react to rude or brash behaviors of others often in the same way to prevail.

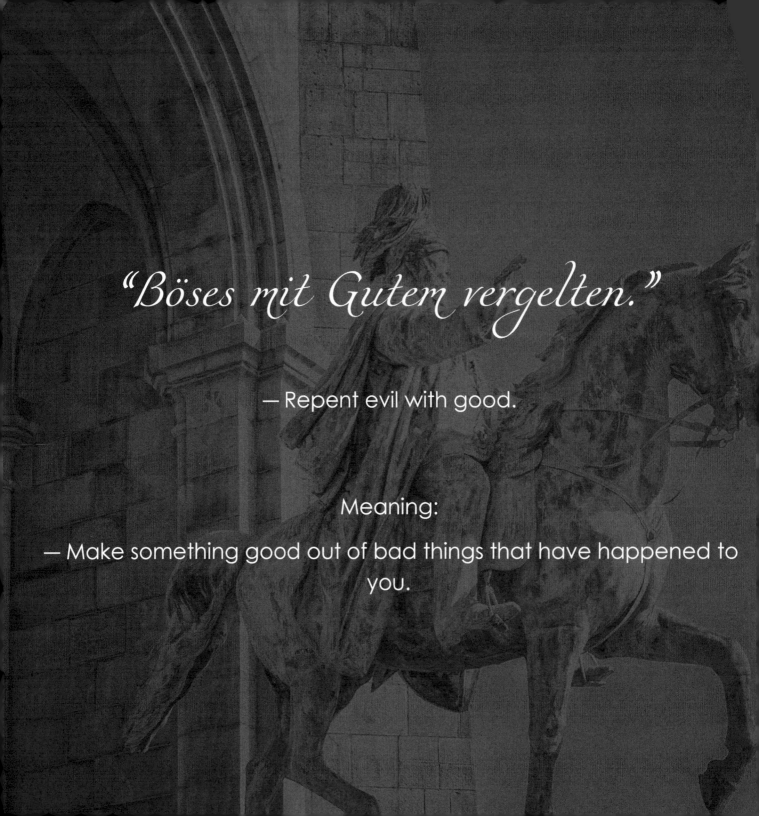

"*Böses mit Gutem vergelten.*"

— Repent evil with good.

Meaning:

— Make something good out of bad things that have happened to you.

"*Deine Wäsche wasche zu Hause.*"

— Wash your laundry at home.

Meaning:

— Don't proclaim your own disgrace, or expose the faults or weaknesses of your family.

"*Bellende Hunde beißen nicht.*"

— Barking dogs don't bite.

Meaning:

— People who make the most or the loudest threats are the least likely to take action.

"Wer im Glashaus sitzt sollte nicht mit Steinen werfen."

— People who sit in glass houses shouldn't throw stones.

Meaning:

— You shouldn't criticize someone if you yourself are the same.

"*Das Leben gehört den Lebenden an, und wer lebt, muss auf Wechsel gefasst sein.*"

— Life belongs to the living, and those who live must be prepared for change.

"Tu nur das Rechte in deinen Sachen;

Das andre wird sich von selber

machen."

— Just do the right thing in your affairs; The rest will take care of itself.

"*Aus den Augen, aus dem Sinn.*"

— Out of sight, out of mind.

Meaning:

— What you can't see won't hurt you.

"*Nur die Harten kommen in den Garten.*"

— Only the hard come in the garden.

Meaning:

— Only the strongest survive.

"Die besten Schwimmer ertrinken"

— The best swimmers drown.

Meaning:

— Beware of letting your competence lead you into overconfidence.

"*Die beste Verteidigung ist der Angriff!*"

— Attack is the best form of defence!

Meaning:

— You are more likely to win if you take the initiative and make an attack rather than preparing to defend yourself.

"*Die Ochsen hinter dem Wagen spannen.*"

— To tighten the ox behind the cart.

Meaning:

— It is important to do things in the right or natural order.

"Die besten Gedanken kommen allzeit hinterdrein."

— The best thoughts always come after.

Meaning:

— Give yourself time to think, second thoughts are the best.

"*Auch der kleinste Feind ist nicht zu verachten.*"

— Even the tiniest enemy is not to be despised.

Meaning:

— There is no little enemy.

"Wie man in den Wald hineinruft, so schallt es zurück."

— Just as one calls into the forest, so it echoes back.

Meaning:

— Do not expect friendly reply when being obnoxious.

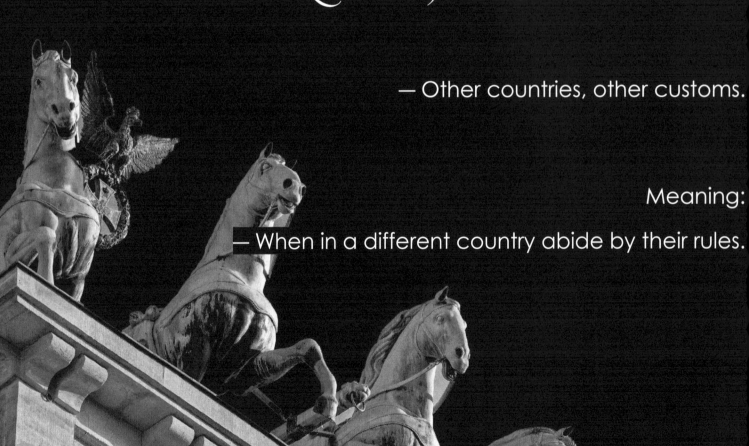

"Andere Länder, andere Sitten."

— Other countries, other customs.

Meaning:

— When in a different country abide by their rules.

"*Wer Eier unter den Füßen hat, muss leise auftreten.*"

— He who has eggs under his feet must tread lightly.

Meaning:

— Know your limitations and weaknesses.

"Geteilte Freude ist doppelte Freude, geteilter Schmerz ist halber Schmerz."

— Shared joy is double joy, shared sorrow is halved sorrow.

Meaning:

— Sharing emotions with someone makes things better.

"Der Schein trügt."

.

– Appearances deceive.

Meaning:

— Things are not always as they seem.

"Die Ratten verlassen das sinkende Schiff"

— Rats desert a sinking ship.

Meaning:

— A leader or organization in trouble will quickly be abandoned.

"Der Fisch stinkt rom Kopf her."

— A fish stinks from the head.

Meaning:

— A corrupting influence often spreads from a leader to the rest of the organization group.

"Wer zuletzt lacht, lacht am besten."

— He who laughs last, laughs the best.

Meaning:

— Minor successes or failures along the way are of no significance — the person who is ultimately triumphant is the only real winner.

"Wer Feuer bedarf, sucht es in der Asche."

— Who needs fire looks for it in the ashes.

Meaning:

— To turn a minor issue into a major source of conflict.

"*Unter den Blinden ist der Einäugige König.*"

— Among the blind, the one-eyed is king.

Meaning:

— People of only limited capability can succeed when surrounded by those who are even less able than themselves.

"Was man nicht im Kopf hat, muss man in den Beinen haben."

— What you do not have in mind, you have to have in the legs.

Meaning:

— Those who do not have their thoughts together are eventually punished for having to travel two or three times to sort out what they wanted.

"Bald reif hält nicht steif."

— Early ripe does not hold stiff.

Meaning:

— Precocious talent or premature success is often short-lived.

"Dienst ist Dienst und Schnaps ist Schnaps."

— Work is work and liquor is liquor.

Meaning:

— Sometimes you have to work hard and get on with it. It can't always be fun.

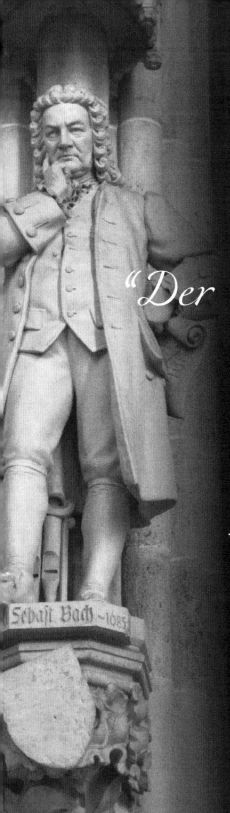

Sebast. Bach ~1685

"*Der Hunger kommt beim Essen.*"

— Appetite emerges while eating.

Meaning:

— One of the hardest things to do is to get started.

After a while it will become habit.

"Harte Schale, weicher Kern."

— Hard shell soft core.

Meaning:

— Used for a person who looks stern on the inside but has a soft personality.

"*Wer A sagt, muss auch B sagen.*"

— He who says A also has to say B.

Meaning:

— If you commit to something, commit to it all the way.

"*Wer zwei Hasen auf einmal jagt bekommt keinen.*"

— He who chases two rabbits at once will catch none.

Meaning:

— Be focused. Concentrate on one thing at a time and then move on to the next.

"*Die Kuh rom Eis holen.*"

— Get the cow off the ice.

Meaning:

— Escape a risky situation.

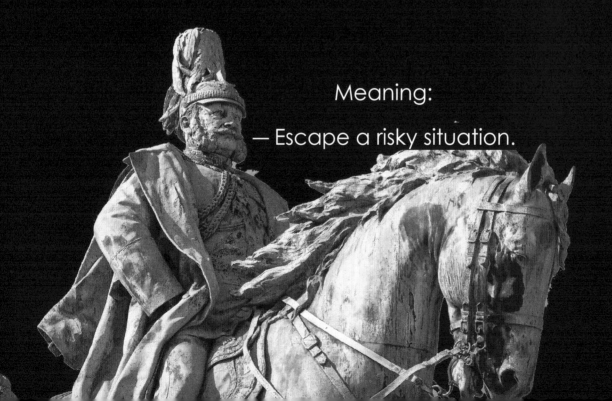

"Wer den Pfennig nicht ehrt, ist des Talers nicht wert."

— Who does not appreciate the pennies, doesn't deserve the coins.

Meaning:

— Little things should be appreciated for big things come into your life.

"Selbst ist der Mann./Selbst ist die Frau."

— Yourself is the man./Yourself is the woman.

Meaning:

— If you want something done, you have to do it yourself

"Morgenstund hat Gold im Mund."

— The morning hour has gold in its mouth.

Meaning:

— Get up early to get a head start on the day.

"Es ist noch kein Meister vom Himmel gefallen."

— No master has fallen from the sky yet.

Meaning:

— Similar to practice makes perfect. You need to do a lot in order to get somewhere, knowledge is not given without effort.

"Krummes Holz gibt auch gerades Feuer."

— Crooked logs also make straight fires.

Meaning:

— Don't wait for the perfect, when slightly less will also work.

"Wer befehlen will, muß gehorchen lernen."

— Who wants to command must learn to obey.

Meaning:

— One must have been controlled in the same situation if one wishes to properly control others.

"*Wenn der Himmel einfällt bleibt nirgends ein stehen.*"

— When the sky collapses, there will be nowhere to stand.

Meaning:

— A little which is good, is better than a great deal of that which is good for nothing.

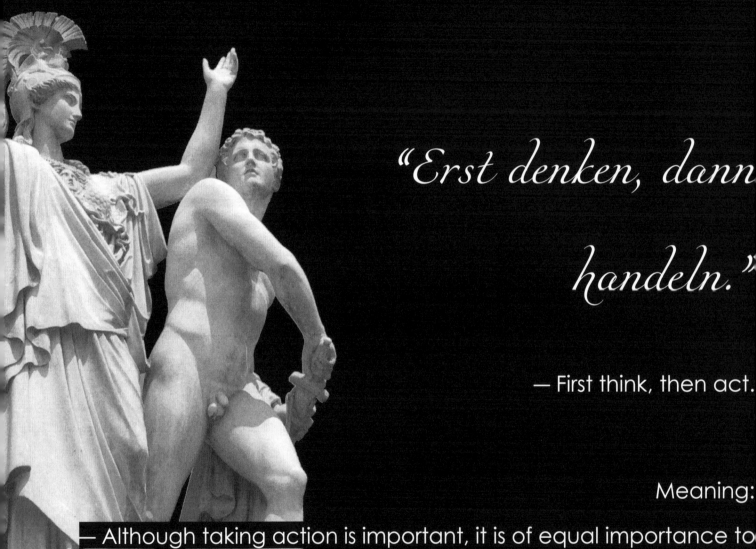

"Erst denken, dann handeln."

— First think, then act.

Meaning:
— Although taking action is important, it is of equal importance to take the right action.

"*Du siehst den Wald vor lauter Bäumen nicht.*"

— You don't see the forest for all the trees.

Meaning:

— It is important to see the big picture.

"Das Billige ist immer das Teuerste."

— The cheapest is always the most expensive.

Meaning:

— This saying is a reminder to invest into quality.

"Verborgener Schatz ist nichts wert."

— A hidden treasure is worth nothing.

Meaning:

— Money is there to be spent.

"Anfangen ist leicht, Beharren eine Kunst"

— Starting is easy, persistence is an art.

Meaning:

— Starting something is easier, seeing it through to the end is the difficult part.

"Wer rastet, der rostet."

— He who rests grows rusty.

Meaning:

— In order to improve your skills, you have to continuously work.

"Aller Anfang ist schwer."

— All beginnings are hard.

Meaning:

— Learning new things are difficult to begin with, so you must keep trying.

"Des Teufels liebstes Möbelstück ist die lange Bank."

— The devil's favorite piece of furniture is the long bench.

Meaning:

— "Long bench" means putting off a task/it's bad to procrastinate/delay or postpone action.

Thank you for your purchase!

We spent a long time building this book.

We hope you enjoyed it :)

If you did please help us by leaving a review...

PS. Join our team to receive some Kindle edition books free and before anyone else...

Find out more on our website here:

www.theSecretlibraries.com

The Secret Libraries

Published by The Secret Libraries for 2017

www.theSECRETlibraries.com

Printed in Great Britain
by Amazon